Orson's Tummy Ache

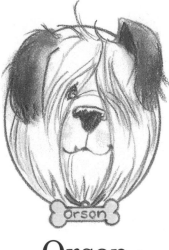

Orson

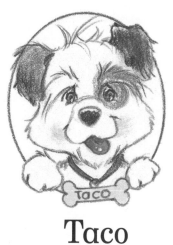

Taco

The big dog ate
a little dog food.

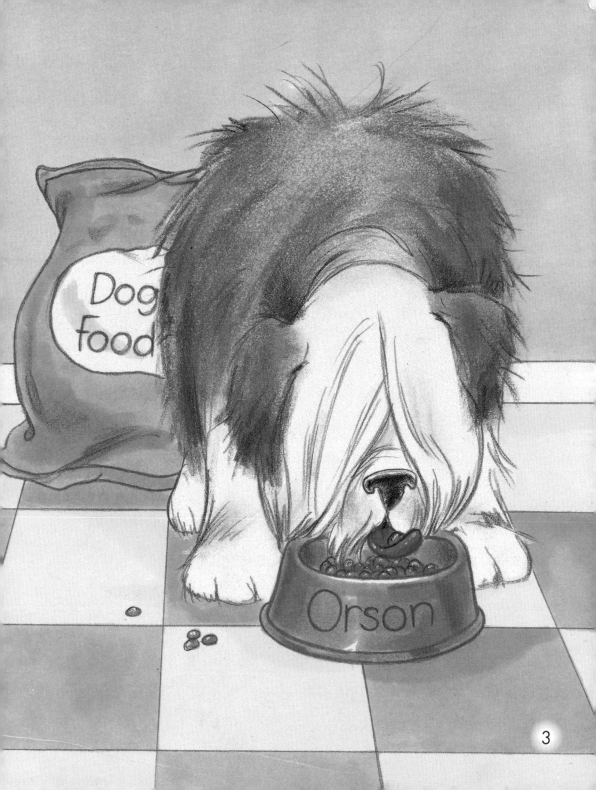

The big dog ate
a little grass.

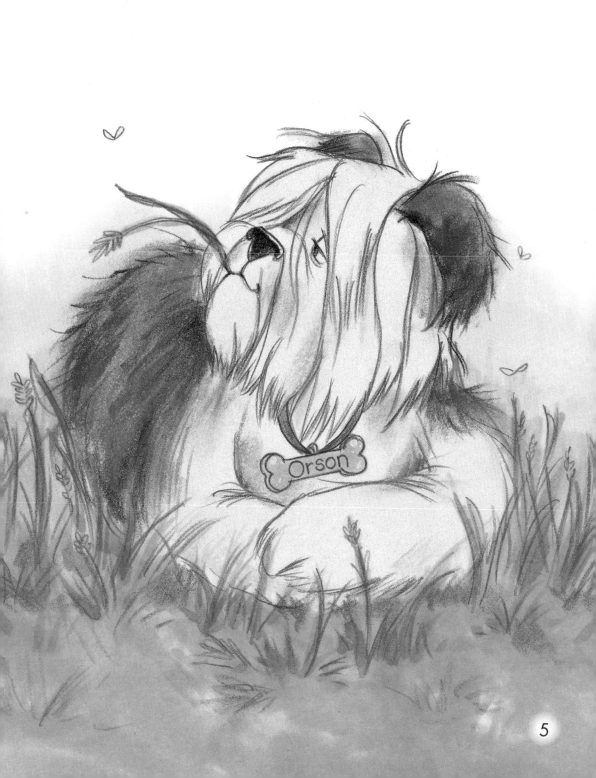

The big dog ate
the big cookie.

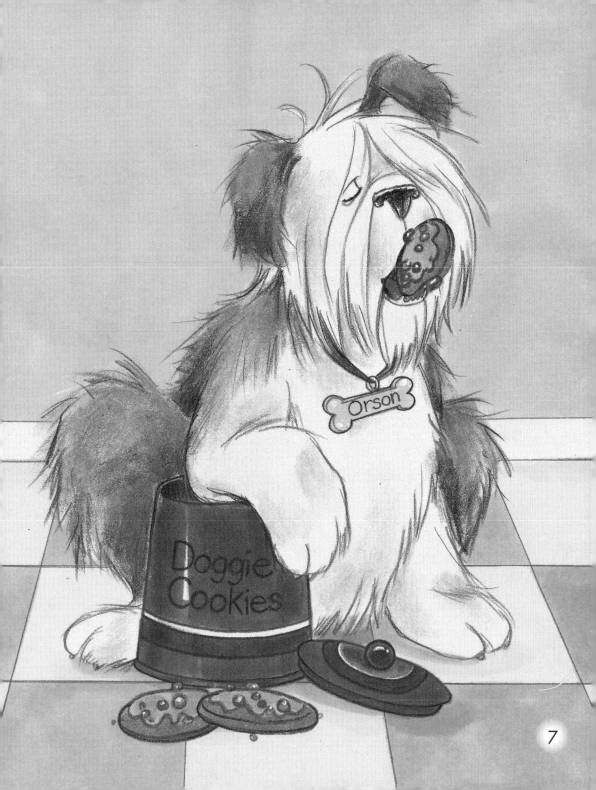

The big dog ate
a little stick.

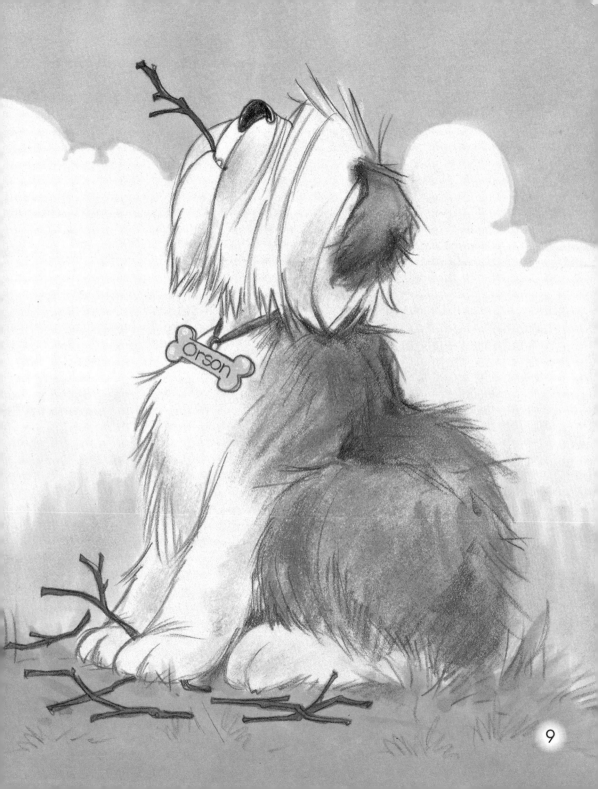

The big dog ate a big bone.

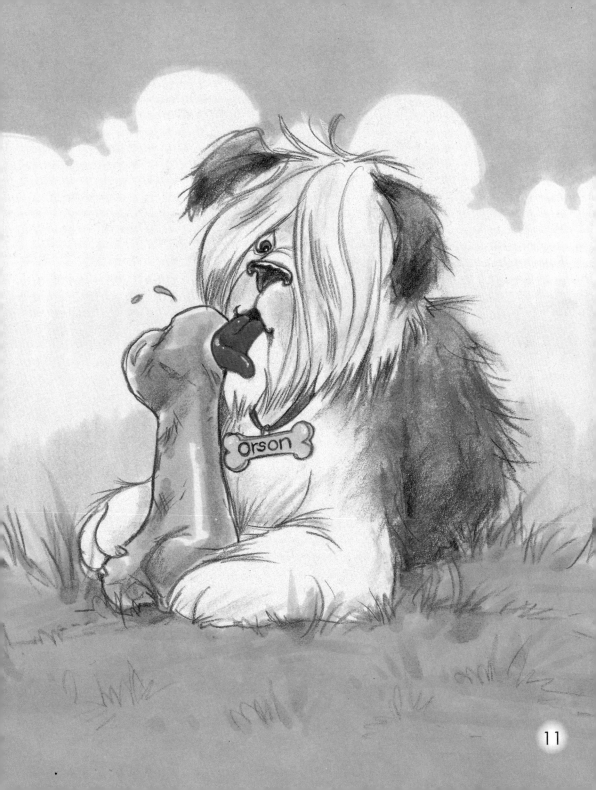

The big dog ate
the little apple.

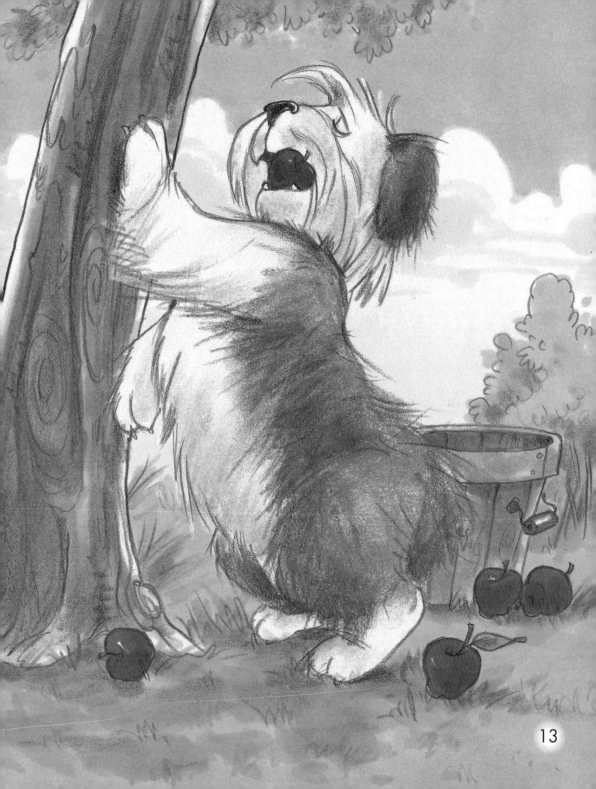

The big dog ate
a little bug.

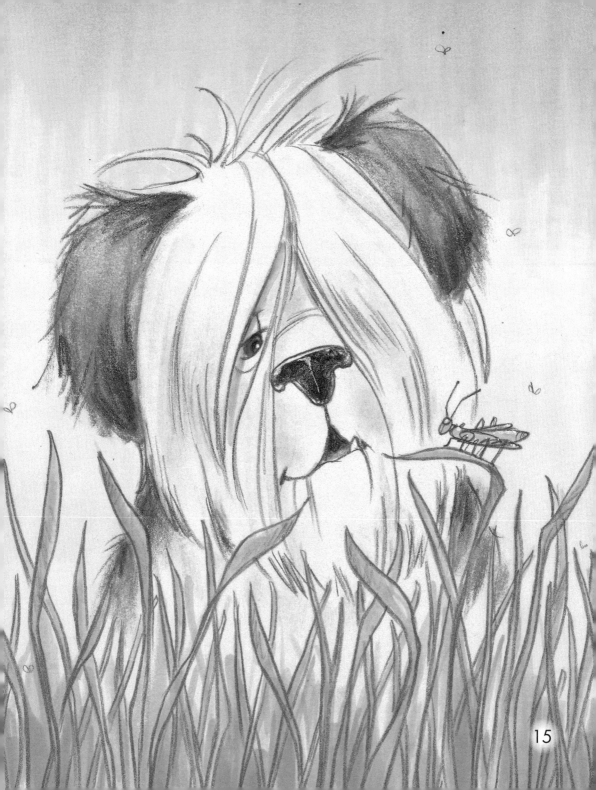

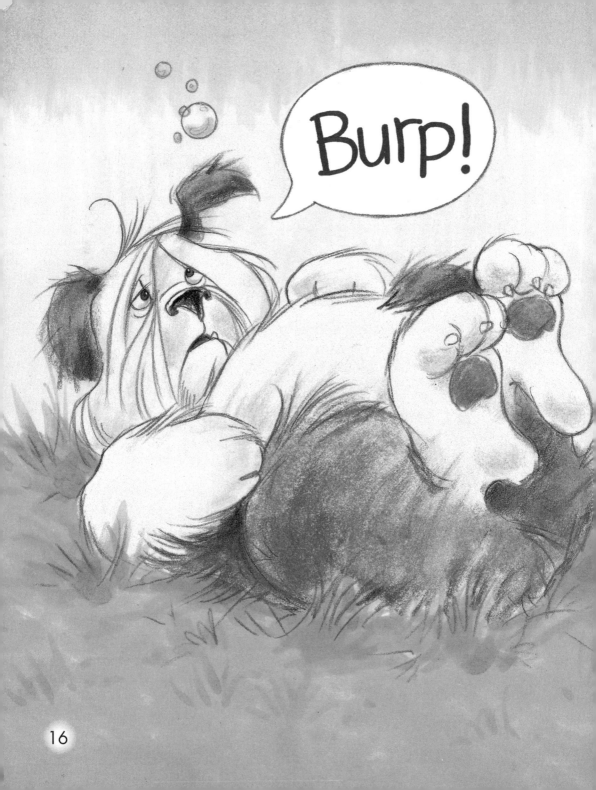